Debating History

DEBATES ON THE SLAVE TRADE

Don Nardo

ReferencePoint Press®

San Diego, CA

© 2019 ReferencePoint Press, Inc.
Printed in the United States

For more information, contact:
ReferencePoint Press, Inc.
PO Box 27779
San Diego, CA 92198
www.ReferencePointPress.com

LIBRARY OF CONGRESS CATALOGING-IN-PUBLICATION DATA

Name: Nardo, Don, 1947– author.
Title: Debates on the Slave Trade/by Don Nardo.
Description: San Diego, CA: ReferencePoint Press, Inc., [2019] | Series: Debating History | Includes bibliographical references and index.
Identifiers: LCCN 2017054320 (print) | LCCN 2018012029 (ebook) | ISBN 9781682823743 (eBook) | ISBN 9781682823736 (hardback)
Subjects: LCSH: Slavery—History—Juvenile literature.
Classification: LCC HT861 (ebook) | LCC HT861 .N369 2019 (print) | DDC 306.3/6209—dc23
LC record available at https://lccn.loc.gov/2017054320

Contents

Is slavery immoral?

No thinking person today would argue that slavery is moral. Yet in the United States in the early and mid-1800s, slavery was an accepted institution in the southern states. While many southerners never owned slaves, the institution of slavery had widespread support from plantation owners, elected officials, and even the general populace. Its defenders were often respected members of their communities. For instance, John C. Calhoun—a US senator from South Carolina—was a staunch defender of slavery. He believed that enslaved Africans benefited from their status as slaves—and said as much during an 1837 Senate speech. "Never before," he stated, "has the black race of Central Africa, from the dawn of history to the present day, attained a condition so civilized and so improved, not only physically, but morally and intellectually."

Statements like this might be confounding and hurtful today. But a true understanding of history—especially of those events that have altered daily life and human communities—requires students to become familiar with the thoughts, attitudes, and beliefs of the people who lived these events. Only by examining various perspectives will students truly understand the past and be able to make sound judgments about the future.

This is the goal of the *Debating History* series. Through a narrative-driven, pro/con format, the series introduces students to some of the complex issues that have dominated public discourse over the decades—topics such as the slave trade, twentieth-century immigration, the Soviet Union's collapse, and the rise of Islamist extremism. All chapters revolve around a single, pointed question, such as the following:

- Is slavery immoral?
- Do immigrants threaten American culture and values?
- Did the arms race cause the Soviet Union's collapse?
- Does poverty cause Islamist extremism?

This inquiry-based approach to history introduces student researchers to core issues and concerns on a given topic. Each chapter includes one part that argues the affirmative and one part that argues the negative—all written by a single author. With the single-author format, the predominant arguments for and against an issue can be synthesized into clear, accessible discussions supported by details and evidence, including relevant facts, quotes, and examples. All volumes include focus questions to guide students as they read each pro/con discussion, a visual chronology, and a list of sources for conducting further research.

This approach reflects the guiding principles set out in the College, Career, and Civic Life (C3) Framework for Social Studies State Standards developed by the National Council for the Social Studies. "History is interpretive," the framework's authors write. "Even if they are eyewitnesses, people construct different accounts of the same event, which are shaped by their perspectives—their ideas, attitudes, and beliefs. Historical understanding requires recognizing this multiplicity of points of view in the past. . . . It also requires recognizing that perspectives change over time, so that historical understanding requires developing a sense of empathy with people in the past whose perspectives might be very different from those of today." The *Debating History* series supports these goals by providing a solid introduction to the study of pro/con issues in history.

Important Events of the Slave Trade

1492
Sailing for the Spanish Crown, Italian explorer Christopher Columbus lands on an island in the Caribbean Sea.

1627
England begins using black slaves on plantations on the island of Barbados.

1538
Portugal begins importing black slaves into Brazil.

1756
The Virginia colony now has 120,000 black slaves in residence.

1500   1550   1600   1650   1700   1750

1502
Spain establishes a plantation on the Caribbean island of Hispaniola; soon afterward it becomes the first location in the Americas where black Africans are enslaved.

1619
The first black slaves in Britain's North American colonies arrive in Virginia.

1776
The thirteen British American colonies declare their independence and establish the United States.

1793
American inventor Eli Whitney introduces the cotton gin, which separates the seeds from the fibers, speeding up cotton production.

1808
The United States prohibits the slave trade, although slavery itself remains legal there.

1850
Between 1.8 and 2.5 million black slaves now work in the American South.

1865
At the conclusion of the American Civil War, more than 4 million black slaves in the United States gain their freedom.

| 1800 | 1830 | 1860 | 1890 | 1920 | 1950 | 1980 |

1888
Brazil ends its participation in the Atlantic slave trade, becoming the last nation to do so.

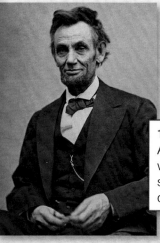

1961
Saudi Arabia becomes one of the last few nations to ban slavery.

1809
Abraham Lincoln, who will later fight to end slavery as the US president, is born.

1807
Britain becomes the first nation in the world to ban the slave trade.

Chapter One

A Brief History of the Slave Trade

The infamous, brutally efficient Atlantic slave trade reached its zenith during the mid-to-late 1700s. For close to three centuries, before it was abolished in the 1800s, this enormous, horrific enterprise captured black Africans and carried them across the ocean to become slaves in the Americas. The general consensus of scholars is that between 10 million and 12 million people were transported in this manner against their will. Possibly as many as a third of them died during the awful journey.

The Trans-Saharan Slave Network

Most of the traders in this vast Atlantic slave project were Europeans or their descendants in the Americas. Yet Europeans neither invented the trade nor possessed the expertise to develop it into an incredibly well-organized and lucrative venture. Rather, they copied an existing slave-trading organization operated by Arabs and other Muslims in the Middle East and North Africa. Beginning in the 700s and lasting well into the 1700s, this trans-Saharan slave network operated with vicious efficiency. The term *trans-Saharan* derives from the fact that most of the slaves this network exploited came from sub-Saharan Africa—that is, the lands lying just south of the vast, arid Sahara Desert.

The trans-Saharan slave trade originally developed partly because Islamic law forbids Muslims from enslaving one another. Eager to find non-Muslim slaves, Middle Eastern slave traders looked further afield, at the many tribal societies living in north-central Africa. Slavers entered that region and either captured groups of locals or bought them from village chiefs. The slavers then dragged their human booty northward and sold them to farm, estate, and mine owners in Egypt, Arabia, Iraq, and other parts of the Middle East. Some of the black slaves eventually ended up serving in Muslim armies.

The total number of Africans exploited in the trans-Saharan slave trade is uncertain. According to scholar Pekka Masonen of Finland's University of Tampere,

> There are no records concerning the volume of the trans-Saharan slave trade, but it is estimated that during the thousand years, which followed its beginning in the 8th century CE, about 9.3 million black slaves were imported to the north, including those who died during the painful crossing of the desert. In fact, the total quantity of trans-Saharan slave trade was equal to the Atlantic trade, though its annual volume was much lower.[1]

An Enormous, Unexpected Wild Card

Late medieval European nations did not tend to use slaves in their own societies, so they saw no need to try to compete with the Arab slave network. That situation changed, however, during the late 1300s. At that juncture, the Genoese (the inhabitants of the Italian city-state of Genoa) speculated that they could make a lot of money by running sugar plantations on various Mediterranean islands. They reasoned that they would need free labor in the form of slaves to make those plantations profitable. Thus, from the late 1300s to the late 1400s they imitated the Arab model and exploited black Africans.

During those same years, the Portuguese saw the potential for creating large-scale sugar plantations on the Cape Verde, Madeira, and Canary Islands (all situated off Africa's northwestern coast). Initially the work was done by white European laborers. But eventually the owners turned instead to the cheaper option of exploiting black African slaves.

During the period in question most other Europeans showed little or no interest in the use of African slaves. But during the late 1400s and on into the 1500s, an enormous, totally unexpected event utterly changed that picture. This was the discovery of the Americas, two gigantic continents that up until then had been unknown to Europeans. It soon became clear that the lands across the Atlantic featured numerous coasts and islands ripe for creating sugar plantations and other large commercial ventures.

The first Europeans who took advantage of this idea were the Spaniards. In 1502 they established successful plantations on the island of Hispaniola, situated southeast of Cuba. At first they tried using local peoples as forced laborers, but within a short time nearly all the island's native inhabitants had been worked to death. Hence, the Spaniards had a choice: exploit white workers or black African slaves. In the words of historian Johannes Postma, "Africans became the preferred labor force" for the Spanish plantations. Only "people who were different," particularly racially so, "were made chattel slaves. In that sense, Europeans acted like Muslims, who enslaved outsiders, or 'infidels,' but protected fellow Muslims from that fate."[2]

The use of black Africans by the Spaniards—based on Arab, Genoese, and Portuguese models—marked the start of the Atlantic slave trade. That insidious undertaking subsequently expanded at a relentless pace. The Portuguese began importing African slaves into Brazil in 1538; the English did the same in Barbados in 1627; and shortly afterward the French entered the

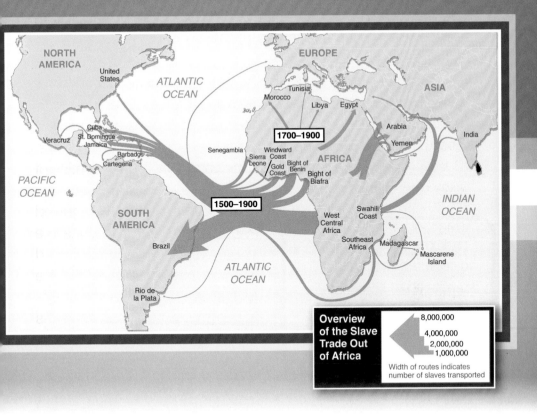

NORTH AMERICA
United States
ATLANTIC OCEAN
EUROPE
ASIA
Tunisia
Morocco
Libya Egypt
Arabia
India
Yemen
1700–1900
Cuba
Veracruz St. Domingue
Jamaica
Barbados
Cartegena
Senegambia Windward Coast
Sierra Coast
Leone Gold Bight of
Coast Benin
Bight of Biafra
AFRICA
PACIFIC OCEAN
SOUTH AMERICA
1500–1900
West Central Africa
Swahili Coast
INDIAN OCEAN
Brazil
Southeast Africa Madagascar
Mascarene Island
ATLANTIC OCEAN
Rio de la Plata
ATLANTIC OCEAN

Overview of the Slave Trade Out of Africa

8,000,000
4,000,000
2,000,000
1,000,000

Width of routes indicates number of slaves transported

trade by introducing black slaves into their Caribbean colony of St. Domingue. A century later the St. Domingue colony alone required the forced labor of some 455,000 imported black Africans to operate.

The Horrors of the Atlantic Crossing

The first black slaves in Britain's North American colonies, the future United States, arrived in 1619 in Virginia. There, most of the Africans came to be concentrated in the southern colonies, where large-scale cotton and other types of plantations were common. As such plantations multiplied in the Americas during the years that followed, the Atlantic trade that supplied their slaves steadily expanded. As it did so, it settled into a series of brutal routines.

The most notorious of those customs were the ones involved with the Middle Passage, the leg of the slaves' journey that took them across the ocean in ships. This trip featured a host of cruel and inhumane practices. They included overt brutality by the slavers, horrible overcrowding, and an unspeakable lack of sanitation—all of which contributed to extreme physical and mental distress among the captives.

Surviving eyewitness accounts detail these horrors in considerable detail. A few observers were African captives who managed to survive the Middle Passage and eventually became literate and wrote about it. Of these memoirs, the most reliable and detailed was penned by Olaudah Equiano, who later gained his freedom and lived in London. He described the appalling situation in the ship's hold, where the shackled captives were subjected to sickening conditions. His narrative states in part that

> "[The slave ship] was so crowded that each [captive] had scarcely room to turn himself."[3]
>
> —Former slave Olaudah Equiano

the stench of the hold while we were on the coast was so intolerably loathsome, that it was dangerous to remain there for any length of time, and [it] became absolutely [alarming]. The closeness of the place and the heat of the climate, added to the number in the ship, which was so crowded that each had scarcely room to turn himself, almost suffocated us. This produced copious perspiration, so that the air soon became unfit for respiration from a variety of [disgusting] smells, and brought on a sickness amongst the slaves, of which many died.[3]

Another description of the awful treatment of slaves in the Atlantic crossing came from Alexander Falconbridge. An English doctor, he made four voyages in vessels involved in the Middle Passage. In a book he published in 1788, he provided a detailed picture of the terrible abuses he had witnessed.

After depicting many of those cruelties, Falconbridge addressed one of the main reasons for the ill treatment of the slaves. He pointed out that the white slavers did not hesitate to commit these terrible acts because they believed the black Africans were essentially dumb animals, totally lacking human feelings. But Falconbridge could see that this was not the case. He witnessed numerous displays of human emotions by the Africans on the ships and described how some were so upset about their captivity that they tried to kill themselves. Some succeeded, he wrote. These incidents, along with others he saw firsthand, prompted him to say, "From these instances, I think, it may be clearly deduced that the unhappy Africans are not bereft of the inner feelings [that white people have], but have a strong attachment to their country, together with a just sense of the value of liberty."[4]

The Triumph of the Trade's Ban

Liberty was an impossible dream for the vast majority of black slaves who were exploited by the Atlantic slave trade. Yet the trade itself was not destined to last forever. During the 1700s, a movement made up of people who wanted to see the slave trade abolished took hold. The abolitionists dwelled across Europe, North America, and elsewhere in the world but were most numerous in Britain.

One of the early heroes of the movement was, remarkably, a former English slave trader who underwent an extraordinary conversion. His name was John Newton. "I hope it will always be a subject of humiliating reflection to me," he wrote in 1787, "that I was, once, an active instrument in a business at which my heart now shudders." He went on, "So many respectable persons have already engaged to use their utmost influence for the suppression of [the slave trade], which contradicts the feelings of humanity, that it is hoped this stain on our national character will soon be wiped out."[5]

Although abolition of the slave trade was at first a decidedly uphill fight, Newton and his comrades persevered and eventually won the day. In 1807 Britain became the first nation to ban the trade. That same year, the government of the still-young United States passed a law that abolished the trade beginning on January 1, 1808. (Slavery itself remained legal in America for several more decades.)

> "It is hoped this stain on our national character will soon be wiped out."[5]
>
> —British abolitionist John Newton

In 1815 the British persuaded the French and Dutch to ban the slave trade. Moreover, not long afterward Britain went further and began patrolling the Atlantic and capturing and sometimes sinking slave ships from the nations still involved in the trade. Finding themselves hunted as despicable criminals, increasing numbers of slavers abandoned the business. Brazil, the last nation involved in the Atlantic trade, gave it up in 1888. Thereafter, the actual institution of slavery persisted in a number of nations (for instance, it was legal in Saudi Arabia until 1961). Nonetheless, the triumph of the slave trade's ban proved a crucial first step in the eventual abolition of slavery itself. Today it is illegal around the globe yet still exists in many regions.

Chapter Two

Is Slavery Immoral?

Slavery Is Moral

- Both great thinkers and the Bible say that slavery is natural.
- Slavery is necessary to Britain's economy.
- Enslaving black Africans is moral because they are inferior beings.

The Debate at a Glance

Slavery Is Immoral

- All people are equal in God's eyes.
- The slaves suffer trauma when kidnapped from their homelands.
- Enslavement of the Africans is cruel and inhumane.

Slavery Is Moral

"The negro race is inferior to the white race."

—Nineteenth-century American thinker and writer George Fitzhugh

Quoted in Africans in America, "George Fitzhugh Advocates Slavery," PBS. www.pbs.org.

Consider these questions as you read:

1. Over the years people have used the Bible to both support and condemn slavery. Why do you think those on both sides of the issue sought biblical backing?
2. How strong is the argument that the morality of slavery is "obvious" or "logical"—and why?
3. Scientists have proved that all humans are descended from the same small group of black-skinned Africans. How does that fact affect the arguments of the slave trade's supporters?

Editor's note: The discussion that follows presents common arguments made in support of this perspective. All arguments are supported by facts, quotes, and examples taken from various sources of the period or present day.

Slavery, and the Atlantic trade that supplies masters in Britain and North America with their slaves, is a perfectly moral social institution. In part this is because great thinkers of the past—both Christian and non-Christian—have declared that to be the case. Among traditional Christian authorities one cannot find one more respected and convincing than the venerable Saint Paul. In the New Testament epistle to the Ephesians he makes it clear that God upholds slavery. Moreover, Paul says, the Lord expects slaves to work hard for their masters, and if they do, they will be rewarded in the next life. In Paul's own words,

> Slaves, be obedient to the men who are called your masters in this world, with deep respect and sincere loyalty, as you are obedient to Christ, not only when you are under

their eye, as if you had only to please men, but because you are slaves of Christ and wholeheartedly do the will of God. Work hard and willingly, but do it for the sake of the Lord and not for the sake of men. You can be sure that everyone, whether a slave or a free man, will be properly rewarded by the Lord for whatever work he has done well.[6]

A later Christian thinker, the great fifth-century CE theologian Saint Augustine, also emphasized in his writings that slavery is a natural condition. He explained it differently, though no less persuasively, than Paul did. Augustine pointed out that because sin

The fifth-century Christian theologian Saint Augustine (pictured) explained the existence of slavery within human society by suggesting that the sins of humanity corrupted the human condition enough to allow the imperfect condition of slavery to exist.

exists among humans, it allows for the existence of slavery. One way of interpreting Augustine's writing is that slavery was not part of God's original plan, but that in becoming a race of sinners, humans opened the door to the imperfect institution of slavery. This is only just, Augustine said. Indeed, "it is with justice, we believe," he wrote, "that the condition of slavery is the result of sin."[7]

Although the great sages of past ages were not Christians (since they predated Jesus Christ's birth), many of them agreed that slavery is an entirely natural condition. The ancient Greeks and Romans, of course, had slaves, and almost no one in their societies questioned this fact of life. To ensure that everyone understood why slavery is natural, however, the renowned Greek thinker Aristotle, who remains widely revered among educated people, explained it. He defined a slave as

> "From the hour of their birth, some are marked out for subjection [helplessness], others for rule."[8]
>
> —The ancient Greek thinker Aristotle

he who is by nature not his own but another's man, and who, being a slave, is also a possession. And a possession may be defined as an instrument of action, separate from the possessor. That some should rule and others be ruled is a thing not only necessary, but expedient. From the hour of their birth, some are marked out for subjection [helplessness], others for rule. [Moreover] the lower sort [of humans] are by nature slaves, and it is better for them, as for all inferiors, that they should be under the rule of a master.[8]

Slaves Are Vital to Britain's Economy

Another reason why the slave trade, along with slavery itself, is moral is because it is necessary from a practical and economic standpoint. After all, without slaves, how else can a plantation owner or other well-to-do farmer make a decent profit from month to month and year to year? Agricultural enterprises of that size are highly labor-intensive. They require the services of dozens and in some cases hundreds or even thousands of workers. If an owner had to pay each and every one of those workers a living wage, he would make very little, if any, profit.

Now it should be obvious to anyone possessed of intelligence and logic that the economy of Britain and its far-flung colonies around the globe rests and flourishes in large part upon the success of agriculture. Without it, there would be nothing to eat and everyone would starve. Moreover, that economy would collapse. This has always been the case in the world's leading nations, and it is certainly so for the British Empire, for the simple reason that it is God's will. Indeed, as noted British clergyman Alexander Campbell stated, "To Britain, God has granted the possession of the new world." We marvel, he added, that "the sun never sets upon our religion, our language, and our arts."[9]

Assuredly, therefore, if God did not want Britain and its colonies to use slave labor, logic dictates that he would have created a different sort of agricultural system, one that did not require the use of slaves. He did create the existing system, however. So it cannot be other than moral.

From this exercise of reason we can see that God expected some British folk to own and operate the plantations and other farming operations needed to keep society thriving. If the owners make big profits, it means they are producing the food, cotton, and other items society requires. At the same time, the system demands that those who are clearly inferior in one way or another should become the slaves needed to maintain a vigorous agriculture.

As for who is "clearly" inferior, all existing national leaders agree that they must be the African Negroes. A recent pamphlet circulated in London—written by an upstanding British leader—makes the case for the necessity of a farming economy that utilizes African slaves:

> Our West-Indian and African Trades are the most nationally beneficial of any we carry on, [and] that traffic alone affords our planters a constant supply of Negro servants for the culture of their lands in the produce of sugars, tobacco, rice, rum, cotton, [and] all our other plantation produce. So that the extensive employment of our shipping [and other vital] manufactures are owing primarily to the labor of Negroes.[10]

Are Blacks Stamped from Birth?

The use of black Africans in agriculture due to their inferiority is part of a larger cultural, social, and ethical argument. It holds that the slave trade and the use of slaves in our society are moral exactly *because* the Africans are inferior to whites. This inferiority can be seen in both the slaves' physical and mental makeup. The noted French aristocrat Count Arthur de Gobineau, examined some black Africans and reported his findings. "The animal shape that appears in the shape of the pelvis," he explains, "is stamped on the Negro from birth, and foreshadows his destiny. His intellect will always move within a very narrow circle."[11]

> "[A black African's] intellect will always move within a very narrow circle."[11]
>
> —French aristocrat Count Arthur de Gobineau

Of course, an important aspect of the Africans' inferior status is that their enslavement is actually a boon to them. Are they not better off under the charge of white people than in the animalistic conditions they groveled in back in their homeland? An influential member of one of America's southern states answers that question with a resounding yes. "When a slave to a Caucasian," he says, a black African "is vastly higher in the scale of humanity than when in his native state."[12]

Indeed, all available evidence suggests that these Africans are more advantaged and happier under their masters' care. Their owner will not allow them to starve or go naked, certainly. An English merchant, Michael Renwick Sergant, summarized this point well when he said, "We ought to consider whether the Negroes in a well regulated plantation, under the protection of a kind master, do not enjoy as great, nay, even greater advantages than when under their own despotic governments."[13]

That Sergant's words are true has been verified by any number of witnesses to the slaves' living conditions on the various plantations. With the exception of the ones who are rebellious, the vast majority are treated fairly well. This is even true during the period in which they cross the Atlantic—the so-called Middle Passage. Sir John Norris, a respected member of Parliament, has testified to that august body that

> they have several meals a day—some of their own country provisions, with the best sauces of African cookery; and by the way of variety, another meal of pulse, etc., according to European taste. After breakfast they have water to wash themselves, while their apartments are perfumed with frankincense and lime juice. Before dinner they are amused after the manner of their country. The song and the dance are promoted. The men play and sing, while the women and girls make fanciful ornaments with beads, with which they are plentifully supplied.[14]

Thus, black slaves are inferior to white people, are necessary to keep national economies running smoothly, and are treated well enough considering their lowly status. For these reasons, one can only conclude that slavery is perfectly moral.

Slavery Is Immoral

"[Slavery is] incompatible with all the elements of the security, welfare, and greatness of nations."

—Nineteenth-century American statesman William H. Seward

Quoted in George E. Baker, ed., *The Works of William H. Seward*, vol. 4. New York: AMS, 1972, pp. 291–92.

Consider these questions as you read:

1. How did the intellectual and philosophical movement known as the Enlightenment influence thinking about the morality of slavery?
2. Why, in your view, did slave traders and slave owners of the era not see their actions as immoral?
3. If you lived during the eighteenth century and a relative or close friend bought slaves, what arguments would you offer to him or her that doing so is morally wrong?

Editor's note: The discussion that follows presents common arguments made in support of this perspective. All arguments are supported by facts, quotes, and examples taken from various sources of the period or present day.

Slavery, and the slave trade that fuels it, is morally wrong. This truth is one of the main lessons of a recent, enormous, and highly commendable turning point in human thinking. It is often referred to as the European Enlightenment. That venerable intellectual movement is made up of top-notch thinkers and writers—most of them British and French. They strongly advocate religious freedom, honest and fair government, the use of reason and science, and, most of all, basic human rights. These rights include freedom of religion, speech, and thought. Also important is the right to be treated with equal respect and dignity no matter one's background or birthplace.

Those fundamental truths revealed by the Enlightenment have shown us that the existing economic and political systems—

which supports slavery and the slave trade—is morally corrupt. One of the key factors that makes the trade immoral is that it abuses people who are effectively our equals. Regardless of their skin color and admittedly different cultural attributes, they are human beings, and the truth is that all humans are equal in God's sight. Moreover, the souls of black Africans are no less valuable or deserving than those of white people. To God, therefore, the slave trade is an evil outrage.

Even a number of former slave catchers and transporters who have worked in the Atlantic slave trade have come to conclude that enslaving Africans is wrong. One of these men, Captain Thomas Phillips, now rightly argues that people should not be judged by the color of their skin. As early as 1732 he stated, "I cannot imagine why they [black Africans] should be despised for their color, being what they cannot help, and the effect of the climate God has given them. I can't think there is any basic value in one color more than another, nor that white is better than black, only we think so because we are [white]."[15]

> "I can't think there is any basic value in one color more than another, nor that white is better than black."[15]
>
> —Eighteenth-century ship captain Thomas Phillips

Inflicting Trauma on Innocents

The slave trade is also immoral because it wrenches innocent, unsuspecting people from their families and homelands, to which they never return. This is traumatic, or very mentally distressing, for the pitiful captives. Often they are seized without warning and taken to strange new lands where they must either adjust or die.

The very act of being kidnapped is traumatic, not to mention the thought that one will never see one's family and friends again. The former slave Olaudah Equiano, who managed to survive a stint in slavery and later gained his freedom, wrote a book about his experiences. In it, he described how, when mere children, he and his sister were kidnapped from their home in an African village: "One day, when all our people were gone out to their works as usual, and only I and my dear sister were left to mind the house, two men and a woman got over our walls, and in a moment seized us both. My sister and I were separated and I ended up in the hands of a slave dealer who supplied the Atlantic slave ships."[16]

None other than the renowned British statesman William Wilberforce has described to Parliament such infliction of trauma on the hapless Africans. They, he said, "are so wrung with misery at leaving their country, that it is the constant practice to set sail at night, lest they should be sensible of their departure." Also, Wilberforce told his colleagues, the slaves' songs are filled with "lamentation [grief and sadness] upon their departure which, while they sing, are always in tears, so that one [ship captain] threatened one of the women with a flogging, because the mournfulness of her song was too painful for his feelings."[17]

The Cruelties of the March and the Middle Passage

Still another immoral aspect of the slave trade and the long captivity of its victims in the Americas and elsewhere is the extreme cruelty of the typical treatment of the slaves. This brutality begins with the manner in which the slaves are marched overland to the ships on Africa's western coast. They are shackled in iron cuffs and collars like animals, given little to eat, and whipped mercilessly if they complain or walk too slowly.

When these unfortunates reach the ships and begin the dreaded Middle Passage, their predicament grows even worse. Their captors are most concerned with controlling the many slaves who are transported on each ship. They maintain that control chiefly through the use of brutal tactics designed to strike abject fear into the captives.

One frequent approach is to wait until all the slaves are on board and then assemble them on the main deck. There, the

This nineteenth-century illustration depicts captive Africans being marched from the continent's interior to a slave ship. During such a journey, the prisoners were shackled in iron cuffs, given little to eat, and whipped if they moved too slowly.

captain singles out a captive at random. The poor individual is tied to a mast and is savagely whipped until he or she is bloody and unconscious. The captain makes it clear (through an interpreter) that such beatings will be given to anyone who misbehaves in any way during the journey.

Furthermore, during that trip the slavers regularly force their chained victims to lie in small, filthy, dark, belowdeck holds. They are jammed in so tightly that they cannot turn over, much less stand up. There is no place to relieve themselves, so they soon become covered in their own wastes. Assertions by British states-man Sir John Norris that the slaves are treated decently on the ships are outright lies.

A Wide Range of Torture Devices

Commonly, the slaves who survive these horrors hope that conditions will be far better when they reach their destination. But such hopes are soon dashed. The cruelties they must endure on the plantations in the Americas and on farms in other lands are many and relentless. A slave who breaks even a minor rule is commonly fitted with a tight, painful leather or metal collar that he or she must wear for weeks or even months.

Torture devices of this sort are sold in many general stores in the Americas as well as in some parts of the British Isles. Classified ads aimed at buyers appear regularly in newspapers. One such ad, which appeared in the *London Advertiser* in 1756, read, "Silver padlocks for blacks or dogs."[18] Clearly, ads like this one equate the slaves with animals, which is cruel and humiliating.

In addition to such collars, some masters use heavier, more painful devices to restrain and punish slaves. Equiano wrote about witnessing slaves who were forced to wear thick metal chains or big iron hooks around their necks. Weighing 60 to 80 pounds (27 to 36 kg), these appliances are so heavy that the wearer must bend forward as he or she walks. Equiano also saw a quite frightening instrument used by a fair number of masters to keep their slaves in line. After he had arrived in Virginia, he became a slave on a local plantation and had occasion to see the treatment of one of the female household slaves. He later recalled that "the poor creature was loaded with various kinds of iron machines. She had one particularly on her head, which locked her mouth so fast [firmly] that she could scarcely speak; and could not eat nor drink. I was astonished and shocked at this contrivance, which I learned afterwards was called the iron muzzle."[19]

> **"My master began to whisper foul words in my ear."[20]**
>
> —An African American slave who was raped by her master

These are only some of many means of controlling African slaves on plantations and other farms. The unlucky wretches also suffer having their teeth pulled out, one or more of their fingers or toes hacked off, branding with hot irons, their noses slit with sharp knives, their arms or legs plunged into boiling water, and, in the case of some male slaves, castration.

Meanwhile, female slaves regularly suffer various sexual abuses. Sometimes overseers are the culprits, but the owners are also commonly guilty of these acts. One enslaved African woman who suffered that way eventually escaped, became educated, and penned a book. "My master began to whisper foul words in my ear," she wrote.

> He peopled my young mind with unclean images, such as only a vile monster could think of. I turned from him with disgust and hatred. But he was my master. I was compelled to live under the same roof with him—where I saw a man forty years my senior daily violating the most sacred commandments of nature. He told me I was his property; that I must be subject to his will in all things.[20]

Considering that slaves are seized and forced into servitude against their will, treated brutally, and even sexually abused, there can be no doubt that slavery is an abomination and completely immoral.

Chapter Three

Is Slavery Essential to the Economies of the Southern States?

Slavery Is Essential to the Economies of the Southern States

- To be successful, the cotton industry requires slaves.
- The South's economy is also strongly dependent on slaves who work in various trades.
- Without slaves working in the fields and in the trades, the South's economy cannot survive.

The Debate at a Glance

Slavery Is Not Essential to the Economies of the Southern States

- Slavery is largely an inefficient system that harms the growth and productivity of the South's economy.
- Slavery hurts the South's economy by making many poor white Southerners averse to doing certain kinds of jobs.
- The South's economy is harmed by its focus on agriculture at the expense of other industries.

Slavery Is Essential to the Economies of the Southern States

"[Louisiana and Texas] grow the same great staples—sugar and cotton [—and] are both so deeply interested in African slavery that it may be said to be absolutely necessary to their existence, and is the keystone to the arch of their prosperity."

—Politician George Williamson of Louisiana

Quoted in Confederate Truths, "Louisiana Commissioner Geo. Williamson Urges Texas to Secede 'to Preserve the Blessings of African Slavery.'" www.confederatepastpresent.org.

Consider these questions as you read:

1. Historians agree that slavery is a type of economic system. In your view, why is that the case?
2. The invention of the cotton gin led to the dramatic expansion of cotton farming and slavery. What is another invention that caused major social and economic changes?
3. The South's manufacturing base was much smaller than the North's during the 1850s, just prior to the Civil War. How did that disparity put the South at a severe disadvantage during that conflict?

Editor's note: The discussion that follows presents common arguments made in support of this perspective. All arguments are supported by facts, quotes, and examples taken from various sources of the period or present day.

Slavery is strongly entrenched in the American South, and there is good reason for this. Simply put, slavery is a mainstay of the region's economy. From the 1700s on up to the late 1850s, the economies of the Southern states have been based mostly on agriculture. Large numbers of Southerners still live on the land in rural areas and work as subsistence farmers. A few of the farmers are rich because they own a lot of land and have quite enormous farming operations. Corn, hogs, and root crops are among the most abundant farming products across the South.

In both importance and economic worth, however, those items pale in comparison to the biggest Southern agricultural product by far: cotton. There has been a steady increase in the amount of cotton produced in the South since 1800. In that year the Southern states turned out only 70,000 bales of cotton; today, in 1860, they produce about 4 million bales per year.

Moreover, the selling price of cotton has steadily increased over time. In the last decade or so alone it has jumped by more than 50 percent to 11.5 cents per pound. A bale of cotton weighs about 500 pounds (227 kg), which means that its average worth is $57.50. Multiply that by 4 million bales and one can see that the South's total annual output of cotton is worth well over $200 million. Considering that an average American wageworker makes between $170 and $350 per year, it is clear that the owners of cotton plantations are extremely wealthy. On their backs, in a sense, the South's economy rests.

The Economics of Cotton Production

It goes without saying that cotton production is labor-intensive. The cotton must be planted, tended to while growing, and harvested. The fibers must then be separated from the seeds and baled. All those steps, plus others in between, require large numbers of farmworkers. It would cost a small fortune to hire wageworkers to fill those jobs; hence, the owners of large plantations utilize black slaves.

Indeed, the economics of cotton production show why this is the case. It takes approximately six hundred hours of human labor to bring a single bale of cotton to market, counting all the steps needed to make that happen. In the long run, it works out to a need for one full-time worker per bale. That this is true in practice is shown by the fact that at present the South produces about 4 million bales of cotton and has almost 4 million slaves.

Because the production of cotton was so labor-intensive, Southern planters chose to rely on slave labor rather than paying wages to free workers. As shown in this 1884 illustration, successful cotton production required many people working at different tasks.

Some people wonder why so many slaves are required for cotton production considering that the industry employs the cotton gin, created by American inventor Eli Whitney between 1793 and 1794. That device, which separates the seeds from a mass of raw cotton fibers in a few seconds, saves cotton laborers enormous amounts of time and energy. At first glance, one would assume that fewer slaves would be needed after the adoption of the invention.

What happened in the decades following the device's introduction, however, was that the cotton industry and its markets underwent huge, largely unexpected growth. Because more cotton could be produced in a given period of time thanks to the cotton gin, demand for cotton increased immensely all over the world. This prompted an American planter to exclaim, "Our cotton is the most wonderful talisman [good luck charm] in the world."[21] Similarly, South Carolina politician James Hammond remarked, "The slaveholding south is now the controlling power of the world." Economically speaking, he added, "Cotton is king!"[22] American planters responded to this newfound prosperity by buying more land and vastly expanding the number of cotton fields. That ended up requiring many more slaves than ever before, despite the labor saved by the cotton gin.

As a result of this increase in the number of slaves, today they make up, on average, around half of the South's population. In some states the proportion is actually *more* than half. Slaves account for a whopping 57 percent of South Carolina's population, for example, and 55 percent of Mississippi's residents are slaves of African heritage.

Slaves in the Trades

It must be stressed that, although a major proportion of the South's wealth is invested in cotton plantations and other large farming enterprises, slavery is further entwined within the Southern economy in all sorts of other ways. A number of black slaves work in the trades, for example, as carpenters, bricklayers, plasterers, and so forth. This was the case as far back as the 1700s, before the American Revolution, and has continued right up to the present day.

An often-cited example is the plantation owned by wealthy eighteenth-century Virginian William Byrd II. He owned several slaves who worked as common field laborers. Yet he also maintained a fairly large group of slave artisans—black men and women who were skilled in various trades. "I have my flocks and my herds, my bond-men and bond-women [male and female slave laborers], and every sort of trade amongst my own servants," Byrd stated. These tradespersons accomplished so many important tasks in and around Byrd's mansion and grounds that he claimed he was able to "live in a kind of independence from everyone but Providence [God]."[23]

Letters written by wealthy eighteenth-century planter James Grant of Florida confirmed that he and other Southern gentlemen owned "tradesmen of all kinds" in their slave gangs. It was a rule among the members of Grant's class, he said, "never to pay money for what can be made upon their estates, not a lock, a shingle, or a nail if they can avoid it."[24] Among the typical jobs these black tradespersons did were those of cooper (barrel maker), carpenter, cook, seamstress, blacksmith, and maker of skiffs, row-boats, and other watercraft.

> "[One should never] pay money for what can be made upon [one's] estate."[24]
>
> —Florida planter James Grant

Most often, these and other slave artisans gained their trades skills through a long apprenticeship process that had begun generations before. At some point during the 1600s, a slave owner hired a free white tradesperson to train a black slave, who for a while served as an apprentice. When that trained slave was older, he would take on a slave apprentice of his own, and the apprenticeship practice would continue.

Helping Local Economies Flourish

Today, as in the past, these slave artisans often work full-time and year-round, in the process saving their masters a great deal of money. That makes those masters more successful and thereby helps local economies flourish. Another rich Florida planter, Alexander Skinner, for instance, had black carpenters who were perpetually working on projects for him. They erected various buildings on his property, repaired older ones, and constructed or mended furniture items and wagons. Skinner also had slave blacksmiths who shoed horses, created metal rims for wagon wheels, and made or repaired metal tools.

In addition, some of Skinner's slaves worked as hunters and fishermen. His favorite fisherman, named Dick, supplied fresh fish for both the master and his family and the master's slaves. "Dick was of great use in the fishing way," Skinner wrote to a colleague in 1772. "We have frequently from eight to sixteen large drums [a type of fish] a day."[25] The slave hunter, Black Sandy, provided deer, rabbits, and other wild game for Skinner's slaves, which saved the master the cost of buying food to feed them.

Many other jobs that make the South's economy work efficiently on a monthly and yearly basis are accomplished by slaves with special skills. Some of them are maids, butlers, body servants, food servers, and other domestic workers. Others do leatherwork, including making harnesses for horses, and work with iron, either as miners or fashioners of decorative metal items. Other slaves labor in the few factories the South possesses or on naval docks and sailing ships.

Slavery Intertwines All Aspects of Southern Life

Thus, several of the main sectors of the South's economy support one another both physically and financially. In fact, all Southern economic factors related to slaves are interrelated in complex ways. Those factors regularly come together, forming an economy based so squarely on slave ownership that without those slaves the South could not long survive. Without slaves to prop it up, that economy would surely collapse, causing widespread financial and social ruin. Therefore, no one of sound judgment can contemplate the American South maintaining its stability, economic success, and the happiness of its people without the existing slavery system. It has long proved eminently useful and completely necessary.

Slavery Is Not Essential to the Economies of the Southern States

"[Slavery is] unfavourable to trade and manufactures, which have ever flourished in free states. [Successful] commerce especially flies from oppression, and rests only on the wings of liberty."

—Eighteenth-century Virginia planter Arthur Lee

Arthur Lee, *An Essay in Vindication of the Continental Colonies of America from a Censure of Mr. Adam Smith, in His Theory of Moral Sentiments*. London: T. Becket and P.A. De Honda, 1764, p. 39.

Consider these questions as you read:

1. In what ways did slavery hinder the economies of the Southern states?
2. Do you believe the large Southern plantations could have operated without the use of slaves? If so, how so? If not, why not?
3. In what ways did the economies of the North benefit from not relying on slave labor?

Editor's note: The discussion that follows presents common arguments made in support of this perspective. All arguments are supported by facts, quotes, and examples taken from various sources of the period or present day.

Despite what many slave owners claim, slavery is not essential to the South's economy. In fact, that institution actually limits the growth and productivity of the economies of the Southern states. Some of the proof for this lies in the fact that the region's present slave-based economy is actually *not* successful, especially when contrasted with the North's economy. In part, this is because the slavery system that props up the large Southern plantations is inherently inefficient.

First, contrary to popular assumptions, slave labor is not free of cost. The slave owner must buy the slave, whose price can

Slaves were bought and sold at markets like the one pictured here. Slavery opponents argued that the system was not cost-effective because the purchase price of the slave, along with the costs associated with keeping slaves clothed, housed, and fed, sometimes outweighed the profits resulting from their labor.

sometimes be quite high. Slaves must also be housed, clothed, fed, and so forth. Every slave owner knows full well that these upkeep costs sometimes outweigh the profits he gains through a given slave's labors, which shows that using slaves is not always cost-effective.

Despairing vs. Enthusiastic Workers

The inefficiency of the slavery system is also the result of the downtrodden, despairing attitude of unfree workers. Whereas free workers possess the incentive and enthusiasm to work at their full capacity, slaves do not. This point was recently driven home by Hinton Rowan Helper in his 1857 book *The Impending Crisis of the South*. Helper is himself a Southerner and therefore knows the region well. This includes not only its strong points but also its weaknesses, one of which, he insists, is the slavery institution. On the lack of motivation of the slaves to work hard, he states,

> The slave toils for another, and not for himself. Whether he does little or much, whether his work is well or ill performed, he has a subsistence, nothing less, nothing more; and why should he toil beyond necessity? He cannot accumulate any property for the decline of his years, or to leave to his children when he is departed.
>
> Nay, he cannot toil to better the present condition of his children. They belong to another, and not to him.[26]

In contrast, Helper explains, "the freeman must produce more than the slave." This is because the free worker has "every motive to render him diligent and assiduous. If he relies on being employed by others, his wages rise with his reputation for industry, skill, and faithfulness. And as owner of the soil, there is every assurance that he will do what he can to cultivate it to the best advantage, and develop its latent wealth."[27]

> **"The slave toils for another, and not for himself."[26]**
>
> —Nineteenth-century Southern social critic Hinton Rowan Helper

The "Political Vampires"

It is well known that the majority of Southern whites do not actually own slaves. Many of these non-slave-owning Southerners are farmers or laborers who live modestly or, in some cases, border on impoverished. This stands in marked contrast to the less than

1 percent of Southern whites who own large plantations that use many slaves. Those few whites are wealthy and prosperous and control both the state legislatures and social institutions, in large part because they successfully use the slavery system to make themselves rich and powerful.

Moreover, the members of this elite slave-owning class enrich themselves at the expense of the vast majority of other Southerners. In fact, the big slave owners purposely keep the less-well-off Southerners ignorant of the true disparity between these social classes so that most whites will continue to support the slave system. Thereby, the wealthy slave-owning plantation owners hope to maintain their fortunes and superior social status. In an impassioned plea, Helper exclaims,

> Non-slaveholders of the South! Farmers, mechanics, and workingmen, we take this occasion to assure you that the slaveholding politicians whom you have elected to offices of honor and profit have hoodwinked you, trifled with you, and used you as mere tools for the consummation of their wicked designs. They have purposely kept you in ignorance, and [have] induced you to act in direct opposition to your dearest rights and interests [and] have taught you to hate the lovers of liberty. [I] appeal to you to join us in our earnest and timely effort to rescue the generous soil of the South from the usurped and desolating control of these political vampires.[28]

An Aversion to Certain Occupations

Furthermore, the Southern slavery system does more than rob the slaves—and thereby the region's economy—of their potential. It also dissuades numerous poorer whites from meeting their own potential as workers, which in turn negatively impacts the economy. In fact, although a number of poor Southern whites do labor diligently to make a living, many steer clear of the great many jobs that slaves ordinarily do. Southern custom has instilled in them an aversion to such work.

The detailed observations of the great American journalist and social critic Frederick Law Olmsted support this view. He toured the American South from 1852 to 1854 and interviewed many hundreds of people from all walks of life. In the acclaimed volume he penned later—*Journeys and Explorations in the Cotton Kingdom*—he describes the attitudes of average, mostly poor and low-class whites who dwell in areas where there are a lot of slaves. "The wonder," Olmsted, says,

> **"Our poor white [Southern] men will not do [jobs that slaves usually do] if they can very well help it."[29]**
>
> —Anonymous Southerner quoted by noted nineteenth-century journalist Frederick Law Olmsted

is that their own demand for labor is not supplied by these [white] laborers. But it appears that where negro slavery has long existed, certain occupations are, by custom, assigned to the slaves and a white man is not only reluctant to engage himself in those occupations, but is [humiliated by those jobs]. [I have been told,] "Our poor white men will not do such work if they can very well help it. [They] work reluctantly and will not bear driving [being forced]. [Moreover] they cannot be worked to advantage [alongside] slaves."[29]

In other words, if owners were to free their slaves and allow them to become full contributors to society, some of those liberated workers would become financially successful. In turn, many poor white workers would not be averse to doing a wide range of jobs they presently avoid. The result would be a much richer and more productive Southern economy with many more employment opportunities for whites and blacks alike. Thus, by keeping millions of people in chains, a tiny group of white owners have, for their own selfish gains, sacrificed the South's potential for true greatness.

Two Economies Contrasted

The reality, therefore, is that the South's economy is very much regressive. That is, it remains mired in a traditional slaveholding system that never changes. The wealthy slave owners never look to a more enlightened future, nor, with few exceptions, do they adjust to new ideas and practices, especially those that do not require slave labor.

In contrast, the North's economy, which does not rely on slaves, is much more progressive and flexible; as a result, it is stronger than the South's economy. Helper affirms this fact in his eye-opening book. The North, he points out, is far wealthier than the South. This, he explains, is because Northern industries and other economic endeavors are more productive than their Southern counterparts. This is especially true for factories and manufacturing. Moreover, the North's more progressive economy can be traced directly to its use of free workers rather than slaves.

While discussing the South's limited manufacturing base, Helper reminds us that the Southern economy is based almost solely on agriculture. He and several other investigators point out the dire facts stated in the country's 1850 census report a mere decade ago. It revealed that between 1840 and 1850 the North leapt ahead of the South in all areas of heavy manufacturing, including large metal items like cannons and railroad tracks. As a result, in 1850 only 26 percent of all US railway lines lay within the Southern states. Also, overall less than one-fifth of the nation's manufacturing sector was located in the South in 1850, and that small share has continued to shrink during the past ten years. One worried Southern politician was recently heard to say, "The North grows rich and powerful whilst we at best are stationary."[30]

Thanks to slavery, therefore, and the regressive economy it created in the South, that region is in many ways living in the past and wallowing in its own lack of self-reflection. Helper sums up this terrible situation, saying, "The value of all the property, real and personal, including slaves, in seven slave States, Virginia, North Carolina, Tennessee, Missouri, Arkansas, Florida, and Texas, is less than the real and personal estate which is unquestionably property in the single [Northern] state of New York!"[31] This bold and shocking statement proves that slavery is not essential to the South's economy.

Chapter Four

Should Slavery Be Abolished?

Slavery Should Be Abolished

- Slavery should be abolished because is brutal and inhumane.
- Slavery must be stopped because it breaks up families.
- Slavery must end because it threatens America's unity.

The Debate at a Glance

Slavery Should Not Be Abolished

- Slaves are property, and a person's property must not be taken away.
- Abolishing slavery will be bad for white people and society.
- Abolishing slavery will be extremely bad for black people.

Slavery Should Be Abolished

"Let us put an end at once to this inhuman traffic—let us stop this effusion of human blood."

—British politician William Wilberforce, 1789

Quoted in Bartleby.com, "William Wilberforce, 'On the Horrors of the Slave Trade.'" www.bartle by.com.

Consider these questions as you read:

1. What arguments would you make if you were trying to convince a slaveholder to alter his or her views and adopt the position that slavery should be abolished?
2. Do you believe that the treatment of slaves is an important argument for abolition? How would this argument be affected in the case of slaves who were treated well? Explain your answers.
3. Should the threat of the nation being torn apart over slavery have been justification enough for all sides to abolish that institution? Why or why not?

Editor's note: The discussion that follows presents common arguments made in support of this perspective. All arguments are supported by facts, quotes, and examples taken from various sources of the period or present day.

The abolitionist movement was born in Britain and France during the 1700s. Since then it has steadily spread across the Atlantic Ocean to the Americas. Its main argument—that slavery is wrong on many levels—has rung true to increasing numbers of decent people, including in the United States. Little by little, person by person, and household by household, people who once accepted the practice of slavery are converting to the abolitionist cause.

One of the most basic reasons why slavery should be abolished is because it is utterly brutal and inhumane. The awful treatment of slaves starts when they are kidnapped and forced to march in chains overland to slave ships. Then, while crossing the ocean, the slaves are treated like animals and packed into tiny spaces with no light and little food or water. Many of these unfortunate individuals die at sea.

Sold Like Animals

When the slaves reach their destinations in the Americas, including plantations in the American South, the terrible treatment continues. For a good many slaves that abuse begins with the humiliation of being sold at a slave auction. Olaudah Equiano, the now-famous slave who managed to gain his freedom, experienced an auction known as a scramble. At the signal of a drumbeat, he later recalled, "the buyers rush at once into the yard where the slaves are confined and make choice of that parcel they like best. The noise and clamor with which this is attended and the eagerness visible in the [faces] of the buyers serve not a little to increase the apprehensions of the terrified Africans."[32]

The horrors of slave auctions have also been described by Solomon Northup, a black man who was kidnapped in Africa and sold into slavery. During the ordeal of the auction, slaves are treated like sheep, horses, or other livestock. Northup later remembered how his captors placed him in a pen with other slaves of all ages and both genders. The auctioneer "would make us hold up our heads, walk briskly back and forth, while customers would feel our heads and arms and bodies, turn us about, ask us what we could do, make us open our mouths and show our teeth. [At times] a man or woman was taken back to the small house in the yard, stripped, and inspected more minutely."[33]

Beatings for the Slightest Infraction

Once a slave settles into life under the new master, he or she is subjected to a mean-spirited set of rules and laws known as black codes or slave codes, which severely restrict a slave's freedom and mobility. Under these rules, the slave is designated as *barba-*

Although some slave owners treated their slaves humanely, most did not. Common punishments included keeping slaves chained up and beating them severely for even minor infractions.

rous and *savage*, labels that allow slaveholders and other whites to treat him or her as less than human. Some slaveholders are decent enough to treat their slaves as they would white servants—with at least a minimal amount of kindness and compassion. But most are abusive and inhumane to one degree or another.

The cruelties meted out by such masters include chaining slaves for part or all of the day, forcing them to wear metal devices that restrict normal movements, and severe beatings for the slightest infraction. In addition, slaves are made to feel like unthinking machines and are forced to work relentlessly most of their waking hours. Northup describes typical demands made on slaves who pick cotton. The workers, he says, "are required to be in the cotton field as soon as it is light in the morning, and, with the exception of ten or fifteen minutes, which is given them at noon to swallow their allowance of cold bacon, they are not permitted to be a moment idle until it is too dark to see."[34] If a slave fails to pick the daily quota of cotton, Northup adds, the person is whipped until blood soaks his or her clothes.

> "[The field slaves] are not permitted to be a moment idle until it is too dark to see."[34]
>
> —Former slave Solomon Northup

The Pitiless Breakup of Slave Families

Abolitionists rightly focus on such cruelties. Yet they are even more angered by what one writer has called "the greatest perceived sin of American slavery." It is, he says, the fact that many slaveholders have "undermined the same family structure that [they] simultaneously encouraged."[35] On the one hand, these slave owners push their adult slaves to have children. Later, however, they often sell those children or the parents. The results are the same: families are torn asunder, and most members of those families never see one another again.

Northup witnessed such a family tragedy in New Orleans, where a man bought a female slave but showed no interest in purchasing her young daughter. Northup recalled that the girl was

sensible of some impending danger, instinctively fastened her hands around her mother's neck, and nestled her little head upon her bosom. [The seller] sternly ordered [the mother] to be quiet, but she did not heed him. He caught her by the arm and pulled her rudely, but she clung closer to the child. Then with a volley of great oaths he struck her such a heartless blow, that she staggered backward.[36]

The unfortunate mother and daughter were separated permanently. One of the first abolitionists to point out this horrible aspect of the slave trade—and of slavery in general—was John Newton, the British seaman who started out as a slave ship captain but saw the error of his ways and joined the abolitionists. He later wrote, "The blood of many thousands of our helpless, much injured fellow creatures is crying against us. The pitiable state of the survivors who are torn from their relatives, connections, and their native land must be taken into account. Enough of this horrid scene!"[37]

A Threat to National Unity

Still another reason that slavery should be abolished is that it threatens national unity. Differences in thinking about slavery are tearing the Northern and Southern states apart. This is especially true in recent years. During the 1840s and 1850s, slavery has increasingly become a wedge issue that is steadily driving the North and South apart. It is true that there are a number of cultural and economic differences between Northerners and Southerners that have caused distrust between those two regions.

But by far the biggest difference is the existence of slavery in the South. Even many Southern writers and leaders openly acknowledge this fact. Recently (in 1858) an editorial in a major Southern newspaper, the *Charleston Mercury*, stated that "on the subject of slavery the North and South [are] not only two peoples, but they are rival, hostile peoples."[38] Similarly, in the North that well-known Illinois politician Abraham Lincoln has made largely the same point, only with different words. "Near eighty years ago," he said a while back, "we began by declaring that all men are created equal; but now from that beginning we have run down to the other declaration, that for *some* men to enslave *others* is a 'sacred right of self-government.' These principles cannot stand together."[39]

The answer to that question is that nothing can justify such enslavement of our fellow humans. This is why slavery has become not only an embarrassment to our nation but also a reason for forced abolition if Southern slaveholders will not voluntarily give up their slaves. In a recent public speech, Lincoln expressed quite eloquently why slavery has become so dangerous to the country. "A house divided against itself cannot stand," he stated. "I believe this government cannot endure, permanently half *slave* and half *free*. [Either] it will become *all* one thing or *all* the other. Either the *opponents* of slavery will arrest the further spread of it . . . or its *advocates* will push it forward, till it shall become alike lawful in *all* the States."[40]

A number of people are sure that if Lincoln is elected president, he will try to outlaw slavery. That surely will cause trouble. As Lincoln's opponent in a recent Senate race, Stephen Douglas, said, Lincoln's and the abolitionists' approach to slavery "is revolutionary and destructive of the existence of the government." It will almost certainly cause "warfare between the North and the South, to be carried on with ruthless venegeance."[41] Considering that such bloody conflict could actually occur in the near future, all Americans should try to prevent it from happening. The most logical way to do that would be for Southern and Northern leaders to sit down together and find a way to abolish slavery before that horrible institution tears our beloved nation asunder.

> **"I believe this government cannot endure, permanently half slave and half free."[40]**
>
> —Political candidate Abraham Lincoln

Slavery Should Not Be Abolished

"The abolition of negro subjugation involves, of necessity, the abolition of white equality. In short, the abolition of slavery is, to the white men of the South, the abolition of their own liberty."

—American physician and slavery defender John H. Van Evrie

John H. Van Evrie, *Anti-Abolitionist Tracts, No. 1: Abolition and Secession.* New York: Van Evrie and Horton, 1864, p. 21.

Consider these questions as you read:

1. In your opinion, is it valid to argue that abolishing slavery was wrong because slaves were someone's property? Explain your answer.
2. Do you believe that white fears of black violence were justified when abolition of slavery was discussed? Why or why not?
3. How would you respond to a nineteenth-century Southerner who expressed concern about what would happen to black slaves if they were freed?

Editor's note: The discussion that follows presents common arguments made in support of this perspective. All arguments are supported by facts, quotes, and examples taken from various sources of the period or present day.

The abolition of slavery in the United States is a terrible proposition for a number of reasons. One of the major ones is that it would go against one of the most cherished of our American liberties—the right to retain one's property. The simple fact is that a slave is a piece of property. Furthermore, a person's property should not be taken from him or her for any reason.

That slaves are mere property of their owners is built into the legal structure of the Southern states. A Louisiana law is a good example. It states clearly that in the case of a slave "the master may sell him, dispose of his person, his industry, and his labor; [the slave] can do nothing, possess nothing, nor acquire anything [except] what must belong to his master."[42]

The Ligament That Holds Society Together

In addition to state laws, the US Constitution also guarantees the right of an American citizen to keep his or her property without fear of being robbed of it by either an individual or the government. James H. Gholson, a Virginia landowner and an upstanding Southern gentleman, has delivered a public speech that dealt with this very topic. He convincingly made the point that the Constitution's Fifth Amendment plainly forbids the government from taking a person's private property. The only exception would be if that person was completely and justly compensated. Gholson reminded his listeners that the Fifth Amendment "was an amendment proposed by the people [and] intended as a monument and protection of *individual rights against Governmental usurpation.* [This noble precept] has its foundations deep laid in the principles of justice—it is the very ligament which binds society together."[43]

> "[The right to retain one's property] is the very ligament which binds society together."[43]
>
> —Virginia landowner James H. Gholson

If the country tries to sever that vital ligament, Gholson said, American society would no longer be worth living in and trying to preserve. Indeed, he went on, without the sanctity of the rule of keeping one's personal property, there would be no government left worth having. The very existence of human civilization itself would be threatened because no one would be able to trust anyone else anymore. There would afterward be the constant threat that one's property could be seized at a moment's notice.

That was the substance of Gholson's argument about the importance of personal property in a general sense. In a more specific sense, he and others have pointed out that slaves are a kind of property that is essential to the continued well-being of the American South. As one orator put it, "Our slaves constitute the largest portion of our wealth, and by their value, regulate the price of nearly all the property we possess. Their value on the other hand, is regulated by the demand for it in the western markets; and any measures that should close those markets against us, would essentially impair our wealth and prosperity."[44]

Harmful to White Society

As Gholson himself would surely attest, all this recent talk of abolition is both repugnant and frightening to Southerners and other decent people in America. Freeing the slaves who presently reside in the South would be a catastrophe of the first order, one that would wreak havoc on white society. Polite white culture would surely be endangered and perhaps even become extinct. If the purity of the white race is to be preserved, and even survive, black slaves must *not* be set free.

If abolition were to occur, white Southerners would no longer be able to make a living because the South's plantation system would collapse. But do not take my word alone for it. Listen to the words of an expert on the subject—John Townsend. The owner of a large cotton plantation on Edisto Island in South Carolina, he recently penned a pamphlet that has circulated widely though the South. Surely he could not have authored such a work without rigorous study of the issue, so his words should be taken to heart. Abolition of slavery, he states, will bring about

the annihilation and end of all Negro labor (agricultural especially) over the whole South. It means a loss to the planters of the South of, at least, *four billion* dollars, by having this labor taken from them; and a loss, in addition, of *five billion* dollars more, in lands, mills, machinery, and other great interests, which will be rendered valueless by the want of slave labor to cultivate the lands.[45]

Such disastrous financial losses represent only part of the problem, Townsend warns. There are more than 4 million Negro slaves in the South. They usually do little harm to white society because, as slaves, they are either chained or watched closely; if they do get out of hand, local militias can take care of them. But this would not be the case if they were freed. In Townsend's words, "the turning loose upon society, without the salutary [beneficial] restraints to which they are now accustomed, more than four million of a very poor and ignorant population" is a terrifying proposition. These former slaves would come together into a massive, aimless rabble and would "ramble in idleness over the country until their wants should drive most of them, first to petty thefts, and afterwards to the bolder crimes of robbery and murder. [Most whites would] not only be reduced to poverty and want

Slavery proponents issued dire warnings about what might happen if slaves were freed. One such prediction was that freed slaves would band together and wage open, bloody warfare on their former masters that would decimate Southern whites.

by the robbery of [their] property, [but] degraded to the level of an inferior race."[46]

The highly respected Southern military officer Henry Benning of Georgia agrees and goes even further in his dire warning. If slavery were ever abolished, he has written, there will be what amounts to open warfare between Southern whites and blacks. "We will be overpowered," he foretells. Desiring to get revenge on their former masters, he states, blacks will attack our homes and slay us in our sleep. "Our men will be compelled to wander like vagabonds [beggars] all over the earth, and as for our women, the horrors of their state we cannot contemplate in imagination. We will be completely exterminated, and the land will be left in the possession of the blacks, and then it will go back to a wilderness and become another Africa."[47]

Abolition Would Be Very Bad for Blacks

Putting the dangers to white society aside for a moment, let us face another truth. It is that the institution of slavery is nothing less than a boon and a blessing to the black race. The reason for this is the well-known fact that these former Africans come from an extremely primitive culture. They possess a low level of intelligence and have no social skills. Hence, they would be incapable of taking care of themselves if they were free and living on their own.

This idea that black slaves must be taken care of by superior white folk is far from new. Our forefathers were well aware of it. Take one of the most distinguished of those founders—our third president, Thomas Jefferson. He regarded slavery as morally wrong. Yet he retained his slaves, in part because he was sure that if they were freed they would fall into poverty and a state of suffering. It would simply be too hard for them to thrive in white society. In a letter to his friend Edward Coles, Jefferson stated,

Brought up from their infancy without necessity for thought or forecast, [black folk] are by their habits rendered as incapable as children of taking care of themselves, and are extinguished promptly wherever industry is necessary for raising the young. In the meantime they are pests in society by their idleness, and the depredations [preying on others] to which this leads them.[48]

More recently, noted Southern military officer Robert E. Lee agreed that slave owners do the black slaves a favor by keeping them enslaved. Without white support, he said, they would degenerate into barbarism and lives of crime and despair. Therefore, abolition must not happen. In an 1856 letter to a friend, Lee said, "The blacks are immeasurably better off here than in Africa, morally, socially, and physically. The painful discipline they are undergoing is necessary for their instruction as a race."[49]

> "[Black people] are by their habits rendered as incapable as children of taking care of themselves."[48]
>
> —Founding father Thomas Jefferson

In summary, the abolition of slavery is an extremely bad idea, in part because it goes against white Americans' rights to retain their own property. The freeing of black slaves would also wipe out the fortunes and savings of numerous Southern white folk. Moreover, abolition would be harmful to the blacks themselves, who would degenerate into chaos without guidance from their white owners. Abolition must, therefore, be avoided at all costs.

Chapter Five

Should the Descendants of Slaves Receive Reparations?

The Descendants of Slaves Should Receive Reparations

- Reparations would help alleviate modern social problems stemming from the legacy of slavery.
- In the interest of fairness, nations that benefited from slavery must compensate the descendants of those who labored for them.
- Other groups have received reparations for systemic wrongdoing; slave descendants deserve the same.

The Debate at a Glance

The Descendants of Slaves Should Not Receive Reparations

- Demands for reparations ignore the fact that many Africans willingly took part in the slave trade.
- Paying reparations to the descendants of slaves is not realistic; the amount could bankrupt whole nations.
- Reparations would set a bad precedent because of the existence of other historical instances of slavery.

The Descendants of Slaves Should Receive Reparations

"Past injustices and crimes against African-Americans need to be addressed with reparatory justice."

—United Nations Working Group of Experts on People of African Descent

Quoted in Caroline Mortimer, "US Government Should Pay Reparations to the African-American Descendants of Slaves, UN Committee Says," *Independent* (London), January 30, 2016. www .independent.co.uk.

Consider these questions as you read:

1. Do you agree with the view that centuries of government-sanctioned slavery have harmed the modern descendants of those slaves? Why or why not?
2. Do you believe that financial compensation would help right the wrongs done during the slavery era? Why or why not?
3. Why do you think some groups have received reparations for systemic wrongs committed against them but the descendants of slaves have not?

Editor's note: The discussion that follows presents common arguments made in support of this perspective. All arguments are supported by facts, quotes, and examples taken from various sources of the period or present day.

Few people of good conscience would argue with the opinion that slavery significantly blights America's past. That awful and destructive institution destroyed untold lives in centuries past, and it continued to shape the lives of those who came long after the practice was outlawed. It is true that over the course of the last century many black Americans have achieved social acceptance and at least moderate economic prosperity. In so doing, they managed to overcome the horrors and deprivations of their enslaved ancestors.

But this does not mean that the negative effects of centuries of slavery have simply disappeared. To the contrary, many African

Americans still struggle against racial prejudice and social and economic discrimination. Moreover, there is no doubt that these problems are a legacy of the institution of slavery.

Based on these realities, several humanitarian organizations have quite rightly come out in favor of granting modern American blacks reparations, or payments to make amends for past wrongs. The highly respected Constitutional Rights Foundation, headquartered in Los Angeles, summarizes the main argument for granting reparations as a way of helping to alleviate racism:

> The problems faced by many blacks today come from slavery and society's ongoing racism. Blacks were uprooted from their homes in Africa and brutalized in America by a system that destroyed the family structure and degraded the individual. When slavery ended, African Americans owned nothing. Isolated and discriminated against, they were denied education, contacts with society, and economic opportunity. Compared to whites, blacks remain in a disadvantaged position and will remain so until they receive compensation and society's racism ends.[50]

The Roots of Racism

The Constitutional Rights Foundation and other advocates of reparations freely admit that they are fighting a hard and at times seemingly uphill battle. One major reason for this difficulty is that many Americans remain unaware that the roots of modern racism reach backward into the long era of the Atlantic slave trade and the slavery institution in North America. This fact is either not taught or not covered in detail in many US schools. American scholar Henry L. Gates says, "Until we as a society fully reckon with the history of slavery in all its dimensions [and] overcome our historical denial of the central shaping role that slavery has played in the creation of America's social, political, cultural, and economic institutions, we cannot truly begin to confront the so-called race problem in this country."[51]

This unwillingness to recognize the long-term negative effects of slavery was plainly illustrated during the proceedings and findings of the World Conference Against Racism, which took place in Durban, South Africa, in 2001. Sponsored by the United Nations, it brought together representatives from almost every nation on the planet. One of the conference's key findings was that

> slavery and the slave trade [were] appalling tragedies in the history of humanity not only because of their abhorrent barbarism but also in terms of their magnitude, organized nature, and especially their negation of the essence of the victims. . . . Slavery and the slave trade are a crime against humanity and should always have been so, [and] are among the major sources and manifestations of racism, racial discrimination, xenophobia [fear of foreigners], and related intolerance.[52]

Most of the African nations that attended the Durban conference boldly and bravely asked the leading former slave-trading nations to apologize for their roles in the Atlantic slave trade. However, those countries—Great Britain, Spain, Portugal, the Netherlands, and the United States—refused. It may be that these nations worried that apologizing might open the door to demands that they pay reparations to the slaves' descendants; if so, they should be ashamed.

> "Slavery and the slave trade are a crime against humanity and should always have been so."[52]
>
> —The World Conference Against Racism

It is as if the leaders of those countries are blissfully unaware of the awful legacy of the centuries of racism that slavery brought about. In the United States, for example, African Americans con-

African Americans tend to have higher rates of unemployment and lower incomes than white Americans. Proponents of reparations for slavery argue that these are only some of the lasting legacies of slavery that reparations would help remedy.

tinue to exhibit higher infant mortality rates and a lower life expectancy than their white counterparts. In addition, American blacks tend to have higher rates of unemployment, lower incomes, and higher rates of imprisonment than white Americans.

It Is Only Right and Just

Another reason why the descendants of black slaves should receive some sort of reparation has to do with economic fairness.

The fact is that several major Western nations, including the United Kingdom and the United States, are economically successful today in part because of their past use of slavery. That institution gave those nations a huge economic boost during the seventeenth, eighteenth, and early nineteenth centuries. Thanks to the labor of millions of slaves, planters and other slave owners in those countries grew fabulously wealthy.

Meanwhile, the societies of the African countries from which the slaves were taken were ravaged. Over time their economies became weak and, in some cases, destitute. The same was true of the Caribbean islands that became nations after slavery was abolished. They all grew poorer as the United States and other slave-owning nations grew richer and thrived. As Verene A. Shepherd, a professor of social history at the University of the West Indies, points out, "Their success was built on the criminal enterprise of enslaved labor, [and] the economic effects of [that era] are still felt around the world today. While the global powers enjoy health and prosperity, the Caribbean states struggle greatly with poverty, illiteracy and public health crises."[53] It is only right and just, therefore, that the former slave-owning countries acknowledge these facts and compensate the descendants of the victims of past wrongs by giving the suffering parties reparations. Shepherd cites some of the grim statistics that support the case for reparations:

> "While the global powers enjoy health and prosperity, the Caribbean states struggle greatly with poverty."[53]
>
> —Scholar Verene A. Shepherd

> More than 2 million Africans were trafficked to the British-colonized Caribbean over two centuries, with more than a million people forcefully relocated to Jamaica alone until 1808. The mortality rate on some ships was over 50 percent, and that of the survivors of those voyages once

the ships landed was abysmal. The Caribbean states seek reparations for these genocidal actions, because these acts are the economic foundations of the strength of the reigning Western powers.[54]

A Painful Legacy

Those who advocate that Britain pay such reparations were among the many who greeted British prime minister David Cameron when he visited Jamaica in 2015. In a speech to the local government, he acknowledged that slavery had caused some awful injuries in the past. Yet he refused to apologize for his nation's part in slavery, nor would he discuss reparations. Instead, he emphasized that the British were the ones who abolished the slave trade, and he said that he hoped his country and Jamaica could "move on from this painful legacy and continue to build for the future."[55]

Cameron's words, though sincere sounding, are plainly not enough. Simple justice and fairness are the reasons why the wealthy former slave-owning nations should pay reparations to the descendants of their former slaves. Yet, as Shepherd rightly points out, those countries "have not yet expressed remorse or presented apologies [or sought] to find some way to contribute to the restoration of the dignity of victims."[56] This is a disgrace.

Precedents for Reparations Make Them Doable

No one denies that the cost of paying reparations to the descendants of slaves will be extremely high. Yet those costs are not so high that the wealthy nations cannot find the money to pay them. In the past, other wronged groups have received reparations.

Beginning in the early 1950s, for example, Germany began paying many billions of dollars each year to survivors of the Holocaust, the mass murder of millions of Jews and others by the German Nazis during World War II. (Germany continues to make those payments today.) In a similar vein, in 1988 the United States agreed to pay some reparations of its own. It began to issue $20,000 each to more than 100,000 Japanese Americans who had been cruelly imprisoned in concentration camps during World War II.

Advocates of reparations cite these precedents and call on the United States and other Western nations to do something similar for the descendants of slaves. "There is international precedent for reparations for war crimes and U.N. support for restoring justice and dignity to the descendants of enslaved Africans," Shepherd writes. The US government, she adds, should aspire "both to identify and seek redress for the wrongs of slavery."[57]

The Descendants of Slaves Should Not Receive Reparations

"All blacks descended from slaves are [already] more than com-pensated for the damage of slavery by the good fortune of living in the United States. Every black in the United States is much better off economically, legally, politically, and morally than any black living in Africa."

—Ashland University scholar David Tucker

David Tucker, "Why the Descendants of Slaves Should Not Receive Reparations," Ashbrook Center, 2001. http://ashbrook.org.

Consider these questions as you read:

1. In discussions of reparations, how important is it that some Africans willingly participated in the slave trade? Explain your answer.
2. What are some other ways, besides paying cash reparations, that nations could help the descendants of slaves? Would these options be more or less beneficial than cash payments? Explain your answer.
3. Do you believe it is fair to hold modern Americans responsible for the slave trade even though they (and, in many cases, their ancestors) had nothing to do with slavery? Why or why not?

Editor's note: The discussion that follows presents common arguments made in support of this perspective. All arguments are supported by facts, quotes, and examples taken from various sources of the period or present day.

The descendants of African slaves should not receive reparations, partly because their ancestors were as much to blame for slavery as the white slavers were. The fact is that village chiefs and other highly placed individuals in African society aided the white slave traders. During the long period of the Atlantic slave trade, most sub-Saharan black societies practiced slavery themselves. In ad-dition to enslaving other black folk, they regularly sold some of those slaves to the Dutch, Portuguese, English, and other whites.

Widely respected African American scholar Kwaku Person-Lynn points out, "Many [African] rulers knowingly went to war with their neighbors, killing millions and destroying entire communities in order to capture fellow Africans for sale. Maintaining power, expanding the economy, greed, and expansionist ambitions were the prime motivating factors."[58]

No Way to Defend African Involvement

A number of Africans were therefore complicit in the slave trade, meaning that they took part in a criminal enterprise, in this case in hopes of reaping financial gains. This means that a number of nations, both inside and outside of Africa, were responsible for the slave trade. Considering that fact, why are modern African governments not expected to pay reparations along with the governments of Western nations?

Some people argue that Western nations, and not African ones, should pay the reparations because the black African leaders who were complicit in the trade were not responsible for their participation in it. According to this clearly hollow, wrongheaded argument, those African chiefs were misled by white slave traders and thereby did not grasp the consequences of their actions. The late African American historian Chancellor Williams confirmed the error of this argument. "Many Africans," he stated, "became enmeshed in the horrors of the trade, knew what they were doing, [and] became as brutal as the whites in dealing with their own kind."[59]

> "Many Africans became enmeshed in the horrors of the trade."[59]
>
> —Historian Chancellor Williams

One of the chief reasons why these African leaders got involved was because they were eager to acquire guns. Those leaders, Williams said, "saw these new weapons of death as the source of the white man's power and the immediate threat to their own existence." So they bargained hard in an effort to obtain as many guns as they

Because warring African tribes sold their captured enemies into slavery, some argue that African nations are as complicit in the slave trade as Europeans and Americans. Therefore, the argument continues, African governments should be held equally responsible for any reparations paid for slavery.

could. They realized that the African nation-states with the largest supplies of guns could potentially "become big, wealthy powers, expanding their territories over weaker black states and capturing [large numbers] of prisoners to be enslaved in the process."[60]

Although African participation in the Atlantic slave trade was wrong and regrettable, it is a sad reality. Person-Lynn agrees, saying, "There is no way anyone can defend or justify African involvement in the slave trade other than [to] acknowledge that it is one of many historical facts that must be faced."[61]

A Lame Argument

Many Americans—both black and white—are reluctant to face this fact, however. When the subject of the slave trade and reparations for it comes up, they tend to make excuses for the Africans who took part. One of their typical responses is that African slavery was more humane than the version the whites practiced; slaves in African societies were better fed and had a chance to earn their freedom, the argument goes. Therefore, their role in slavery was not as heinous as that of white slave traders. What is behind this lame argument? Scholar James D. Perry provides this answer:

One problem for many African Americans, in particular, is that it is always difficult to acknowledge that one's own people were complicit in wrongdoing. We see this again and again in our work, as people freely acknowledge the horrors of the slave trade, but are reluctant to embrace the truth that their own [ancestors] were probably involved in the slave trade, as well.[62]

There is another reason why many modern black writers—and the white writers who agree with them—are often loath to admit that Africans played a key role in the slave trade. Namely, acknowledging that role negates the commonly accepted myth that enslaving blacks was motivated primarily by white racism. That falsehood persists, Perry explains,

because it is a convenient way of understanding the past and of explaining the truth that the burden of these historical events and their legacy has fallen to black people to bear. Likewise, it is convenient to believe that the blame for slavery can be allotted on the basis of race. This mythology not only allows for the demonization of white people historically, but it provides ammunition for claims of reparations for slavery.[63]

A Fantastically Huge Amount

Yet paying reparations for the evils of the slave trade is enormously impractical. To be more specific, it is too expensive, even for wealthy nations like the United Kingdom and the United States. University of Connecticut scholar Thomas Craemer has studied this issue in minute detail. With the help of some highly complex calculations, he has determined what amounts would need to be paid to the descendants of the slaves of yesteryear. He has published his findings in the prestigious journal *Social Science Quarterly*.

Therein, Craemer explains how he arrived at a fair overall figure that the former slave-trading nations would need to produce if they were to agree to pay reparations. First, he figured out how many hours slaves worked in a typical day, week, and year in the United States between the years 1776 and 1865. (That was the period from the nation's founding to the emancipation of the slaves; in other words, it was the era in which the country allowed slavery to exist.) Craemer multiplied the amount of time that the slaves worked by the average wages that nonslaves earned during that period. He then added in an interest rate of 3 percent per year to account for the rise of prices over time.

Using these and other calculations, Craemer provided an estimate of the amount of reparation that would need to be paid if they were to be calculated and distributed fairly. The cost for the United States alone, he revealed, would be somewhere between $5.9 trillion and $14.2 trillion. Clearly, paying that amount would almost bankrupt the country. Why? Consider that in 2016 the total US budget—the amount needed to run the country— was between $3.5 trillion and $4 trillion. Where would the United States get the fantastically huge amount of money needed to pay reparations? The answer is clear: nowhere. It would simply not be economically feasible.

A Bad Example for the Future

Still another reason why the major Western nations should not pay reparations to the descendants of slaves is because it would set an exceedingly bad precedent, or example for the future. After all, the Atlantic slave trade, which no one denies was horrific, was not the only enterprise of its kind. There were several other historical instances of slave trades and the slavery institutions they fueled. According to noted British historian John MacKenzie, "Setting a precedent through the Atlantic slave trade would raise issues about other slave trades, such as the extensive Indian Ocean trades from Africa to the Middle East and Asia, which lasted from the 1600s to the late 19th century. Some of this trade was to the plantations of Indian Ocean islands such as Zanzibar."[64]

The problem is that if one pays reparations for the Atlantic slave trade, the descendants of the victims of those other slave trades would surely demand that they be paid as well. "Paying reparations for the Atlantic slave trade," MacKenzie warns, "would open a Pandora's box in which the victims of these other slave trades would also need compensation."[65] Where, one must ask, would it all end? Saddled with such gigantic payments, the major Western nations might well face economic ruin. How is it logical or fair to compensate for the ravages of slavery in the past by causing similar economic devastation today?

Source Notes

Chapter One: A Brief History of the Slave Trade

1. Pekka Masonen, "Trans-Saharan Trade and the West African Discovery of the Mediterranean World," Nordic Society for Middle Eastern Studies. https://org.uib.no/smi.
2. Johannes Postma, *The Atlantic Slave Trade*. Westport, CT: Greenwood, 2005, pp. 30–31.
3. Quoted in International Slavery Museum, "Olaudah Equiano: Life On Board." www.liverpoolmuseums.org.uk.
4. Alexander Falconbridge, *Account of the Slave Trade on the Coast of Africa*. London: J. Phillips, 1788, p. 32.
5. Quoted in Spartacus International, "John Newton." http://spartacus-educational.com.

Chapter Two: Is Slavery Immoral?

6. Ephesians 6:5–9.
7. Augustine, *City of God*, book 19, trans. Marcus Dods, New Advent. www.newadvent.org.
8. Aristotle, *Politics*, trans. Benjamin Jowett, in *The Complete Works of Aristotle*, vol. 2., ed. Jonathan Barnes. Princeton, NJ: Princeton University Press, 1984, pp. 1989–90.
9. Quoted in Project Gutenberg, "The Empire on Which the Sun Never Sets." http://self.gutenberg.org.
10. Quoted in Abolition Project, "National Benefits." http://gallery.nen.gov.uk.
11. Quoted in Howard Zinn, *A People's History of the United States*. New York: HarperCollins, 2005, p. 25.
12. Quoted in Stephen G. Hyslop, *Eyewitness to the Civil War*. Washington, DC: National Geographic, 2006, p. 24.
13. Quoted in Abolition Project, "Arguments and Justifications." http://abolition.e2bn.org.
14. Quoted in Bartleby.com, "William Wilberforce, 'On the Horrors of the Slave Trade.'" www.bartleby.com.
15. Quoted in Abolition Project, "Captain Thomas Phillips—of Equal Value." http://gallery.nen.gov.uk.

16. Quoted in Abolition Project, "Olaudah Equiano: The Former Slave, Seaman, and Writer." http://abolition.e2bn.org.
17. Quoted in Bartleby.com, "William Wilberforce, 'On the Horrors of the Slave Trade.'"
18. Quoted in Anne C. Bailey, *African Voices of the Atlantic Slave Trade*. Boston: Beacon, 2006, p. 142.
19. Quoted in Arna Bontemps, ed., *Great Slave Narratives*. Boston: Beacon, 1969, p. 76.
20. Linda Brent, *Incidents in the Life of a Slave Girl, Part 1*, Full Books. www.fullbooks.com.

Chapter Three: Is Slavery Essential to the Economies of the Southern States?

21. Quoted in John McCardell, *The Idea of a Southern Nation: Southern Nationalists and Southern Nationalism, 1830–1860*. New York: Norton, 1979, p. 134.
22. Quoted in Causes of the Civil War, "Cotton Is King: Speech by Sen. James Henry Hammond of South Carolina to the United States Senate, March 4, 1858." http://civilwarcauses.org.
23. Quoted in Daniel C. Littlefield, "The Varieties of Slave Labor," National Humanities Center. http://nationalhumanitiescenter .org.
24. Quoted in Littlefield, "The Varieties of Slave Labor."
25. Quoted in Littlefield, "The Varieties of Slave Labor."
26. Hinton Rowan Helper, *The Impending Crisis of the South*, Documenting the American South. http://docsouth.unc.edu.
27. Helper, *The Impending Crisis of the South*.
28. Quoted in Digital History, "Hinton Rowan Helper on the Impending Crisis of the South." www.digitalhistory.uh.edu.
29. Frederick Law Olmsted, *Journeys and Explorations in the Cotton Kingdom*. London: Sampson Low, 1861, pp. 112–13.
30. Quoted in Helper, *The Impending Crisis of the South*.
31. Quoted in Helper, *The Impending Crisis of the South*.

Chapter Four: Should Slavery Be Abolished?

32. Quoted in Paul Edwards, ed., *Equiano's Travels*. Long Grove, IL: Waveland Press, 2006, p. 29.

33. Quoted in Constitutional Rights Foundation, "Slavery in the American South." www.crf-usa.org.

34. Quoted in Constitutional Rights Foundation, "Slavery in the American South."

35. James McPherson, *Battle Cry of Freedom: The Civil War Era*. New York: Oxford University Press, 2003, p. 37.

36. Quoted in Constitutional Rights Foundation, "Slavery in the American South."

37. Quoted in Thomas Howard, ed., *Black Voyage: Eyewitness Accounts of the Atlantic Slave Trade*. Boston: Little, Brown, 1971, p. 209.

38. Quoted in John McCardell, *The Idea of a Southern Nation: Southern Nationalists and Southern Nationalism*. New York: Norton, 1979, pp. 270–71.

39. Quoted in Abraham Lincoln Historical Society, "Speech on the Kansas Nebraska Act at Peoria, Illinois, 1854." www .abraham-lincoln-history.org.

40. Abraham Lincoln, "House Divided Speech," Abraham Lincoln Online. www.abrahamlincolnonline.org.

41. Quoted in Roy C. Basler, ed., *The Collected Works of Abraham Lincoln*, vol. 3. New Brunswick, NJ: Rutgers University Press, 1953, p. 111.

42. Quoted in Constitutional Rights Foundation, "Slavery in the American South."

43. Quoted in Encyclopedia Virginia, "Speech by James H. Gholson to the House of Delegates (January 12, 1832)." www .encyclopediavirginia.org.

44. Quoted in Encyclopedia Virginia, "Speech by James H. Gholson to the House of Delegates (January 12, 1832)."

45. Quoted in Gordon Rhea, "Why Non-Slave-Holding Southerners Fought," Civil War Trust. www.civilwar.org.

46. Quoted in Rhea, "Why Non-Slave-Holding Southerners Fought."

47. Quoted in Rhea, "Why Non-Slave-Holding Southerners Fought."

48. Quoted in Founders Online, "Thomas Jefferson to Edward Coles, 25 August 1814." https://founders.archives.gov.

49. Quoted in Adam Serwer, "The Myth of the Kindly General Lee," *Atlantic*, June 4, 2017. www.theatlantic.com.

Chapter Five: Should the Descendants of Slaves Receive Reparations?

50. Constitutional Rights Foundation, "Reparations for Slavery?" www.crf-usa.org.
51. Quoted in Postma, *The Atlantic Slave Trade*, p. 83.
52. World Conference Against Racism, Racial Discrimination, Xenophobia, and Related Intolerance, "Report of the World Conference Against Racism," United Nations, 2001. www.un.org.
53. Verene A. Shepherd, "Justice Requires Former Colonists Pay Reparations," *New York Times*, October 8, 2015. www.nytimes.com.
54. Shepherd, "Justice Requires Former Colonists Pay Reparations."
55. Quoted in Rowena Mason, "Jamaica Should 'Move On from Painful Legacy of Slavery,' says Cameron," *Guardian* (Manchester, UK), September 30, 2015. www.theguardian.com.
56. Shepherd, "Justice Requires Former Colonists Pay Reparations."
57. Shepherd, "Justice Requires Former Colonists Pay Reparations."
58. Kwaku Person-Lynn, "African Involvement in the Atlantic Slave Trade." http://raceandhistory.com.
59. Chancellor Williams, *The Destruction of Black Civilization*. Chicago: Third World, 1987, p. 252.
60. Williams, *The Destruction of Black Civilization*, p. 252.
61. Person-Lynn, "African Involvement in the Atlantic Slave Trade."
62. James D. Perry, "Reparations and African Complicity in the Slave Trade," *Traces of the Trade*, April 30, 2010. www.tracesofthetrade.org.
63. Perry, "Reparations and African Complicity in the Slave Trade."
64. John MacKenzie, "Reparations for Britain's Atlantic Slave Trade Would Be Impracticable," *New York Times*, October 8, 2015. www.nytimes.com.
65. MacKenzie, "Reparations for Britain's Atlantic Slave Trade Would Be Impracticable."

For Further Research

Books

Tom Feelings, *Middle Passage: White Ships/Black Cargo*. New York: Dial, 2018.

Sarah Goldy-Brown, *Reparations for Slavery: The Fight for Compensation*. Farmington Hills, MI: Lucent, 2018.

Pamela D. Toler, *Transatlantic Slave Networks*. New York: Cavendish Square, 2017.

Prisha Vyas, *The Economic Benefits and Negative Consequences of Slavery in the U.S.* Charleston, SC: Amazon Digital Services, 2017.

Richard Worth, *Life as a Slave*. Berkeley Heights, NJ: Enslow, 2016.

Internet Sources

Constitutional Rights Foundation, "Slavery in the American South." www.crf-usa.org/black-history-month/slavery-in-the-american -south.

Tibor Machan, "Why Exactly Is Slavery Wrong?," Daily Bell, July 10, 2013. www.thedailybell.com/editorials/tibor-machan-why-exactly-is-slavery-wrong.

PBS, "Living Africans Thrown Overboard," Africans in America. www.pbs.org/wgbh/aia/part1/1h280.html.

James D. Perry, "Reparations and African Complicity in the Slave Trade," *Traces of the Trade*, April 30, 2010. www.tracesofthe trade.org/news/2010/04/reparations-and-african-complicity-in -the-slave-trade.

Verene A. Shepherd, "Justice Requires Former Colonists Pay Reparations," *New York Times*, October 8, 2015. www.ny times.com/roomfordebate/2015/10/08/are-transatlantic-slave -trade-reparations-due/justice-requires-former-colonialists-pay -reparations.

Websites

Abolition Project (http://abolition.e2bn.org). One of the best slavery resources on the Internet, this site has overviews of many aspects of slavery, along with biographical information on individual abolitionists, images, timelines, audio files, and much more.

Civil War Trust (www.civilwar.org). The Civil War Trust's collection of documents entitled "The Gathering Storm: The Coming of the American Civil War" examines the reasons for the conflict—including the leading one, slavery—each explored in a separate link.

International Slave Museum (www.liverpoolmuseums.org.uk /ism/slavery/middle_passage). This extensive online site based in Liverpool, England, includes a section entitled "Life on Board Slave Ships." Links are provided for most aspects of the slave trade and the Middle Passage, including the triangle trade, the destinations of the captives, and first-person accounts.

Making Amends (www.npr.org/programs/specials/racism/010 827.reparations.html). Hosted by National Public Radio, this highly informative website includes links to numerous aspects of the reparations debate, including audio recordings of radio interviews, journal articles, public opinion polls, and more.

Recovered Histories (www.recoveredhistories.org). This intriguing site presents a variety of narratives on slavery. The section entitled "Enslavement in the Caribbean" offers a brief but informative background on slavery in the Americas and then provides numerous links to original publications containing eyewitness accounts of participants in Caribbean slavery.

Index

About the Author

Historian and award-winning author Don Nardo has written or edited numerous books for young adults about the development of the modern world. These include volumes on the late medieval period, the age of exploration, the settlement of the North American colonies, the Atlantic slave trade, colonialism, and the struggles of Native American peoples. Mr. Nardo, who also composes and arranges orchestral music, lives with his wife, Christine, in Massachusetts.